*Fingers of Hermes*

Fingers of Hermes

*Poems by*
Radcliffe Squires

Ann Arbor
*The University of Michigan Press*

A number of these poems have previously appeared
in the following journals:
*Accent, Arbor, Generation, Inland,*
*New Mexico Quarterly, The New Republic,*
*The Paris Review, Poetry.*
"Extinct Lions" was previously published in
*Best Poems of 1955: Borestone Mountain Poetry Awards,* 1956,
Stanford University Press.

Book design by Quentin Fiore

*For Eileen*

# Contents

*Fingers of Hermes*

## Extinct Lions

Where lions are extinct you will see some afternoon—
Some lion's afternoon, that is—the golden web
Of the lion's face smiling at you from an ordinary lane.
You will watch him stretch the lazy fluting of his ribs
And soar into a wall of leaves. You may not see him again.

Is it true that the lion stood like an ember in your eyes?
Or, that years ago the last lion died toothless in his lair
Beyond back valleys where his skeleton still lies
Half clasped in loam, half clasping loam in the bare
And loveless bones? You ask this, yet would you tease

The savage body forth unless with a severed will
You were thinking of the time you will break through the wall
Of leaves and into forests where extinct lions prowl,
Even as you mark time with the somnolent guile
Of passenger pigeons, cooing of the sangreal?

# Day-Love

When day-love breaks, the yellow eagle rides
Upon the crimson miasma of a dying flower.
Across the desert jeweled amoebas glide
To meet and merge, to marry and devour,
As the eagle falls like a dusty rainbow on the bride.

In the nests of stone, among the bowers of
Dry petals; oh, truly, within the pastures
Of the eagle, I tell you there is a grove—
At the heart of incandescence, a green vesture
Where daylight is hidden from day, and day-love from love.

Here leaves fall, sleep gathers, but from the black
And subterranean temple the white breath of druids
Sighs up into the ponderous chambers of the oak,
Spilling in green runes from the swaying lute.
We stand where leaves fall, or fall to the eagle's beak.

# Summer Storms

Granite has a face of mere memory, and so insanely pure
Is the memory that at times the world seems to humor it
With long summer rains that swell the meadows to a dour
Tundra. Through boreal mists, tufts of coptis float
As a languid announcement that the ice-age is here.

These storms repent as slowly as ideas. Blue starfish may
Appear in clouds, and saffron lines of light
Take soundings, but the rains return, and angrily.
Even when the sky breaks and the ice-age retreats,
Shadows of clouds brush dusk across the nervous day.

The cloud shadows! Birds drowse and fall to wan
Night twitters. White moths stir up from nowhere to churn
The dusk. And you wait until you feel the day come on
Again. Then as if you were the soldiers in Xenophon,
Who did not gain the sea, you whisper blankly, "The sun."

That was your last autumn. Your last spring
I also remember. The wild dogs sang
In the troubled night; by day they cut
The heavy does from the herd. A rich man bought
Your house, and you were turned out to browse
On dreamy charity's frost-blackened grass.
One wet day we found you planting trees
On our hilltop we had thought an isle of Greece.
And you had bedded field flowers there in rows
And lined up stones like the rooms of a house.
And all was arranged save one small wilderness
Of thorn. Your words, like dropsical flesh,
Will not retract. "I'll leave that place," you said,
"There's someone's grave under the weeds."

In my literal heart I knew there was no grave,
But in the heart that had to have
This hill an island, I felt the roots
Of the stubborn skeleton growing about
Its sacred earth, with an earnestness
Where the breeding flowers have no business
To come and simper. And though I build
A city on this island, Clara, a small field
Will remain merely freighted with earth,
To thank you for your lie and your truth.

## Two Children

There's nothing so sad and sick
As children who are adults. Their hearts
Are swept beneath the rug.
Housebroke, they sit in quiet chairs,
Refusing second desserts,
And grow daft pearls around their fears.

There's nothing so sad and fierce
As children who are children. They war
To take your place,
Pushing you toward your death
Exactly as far
As they are from their birth.

# Epistle to W. M.

The day becomes half evening, half rain.
A lost plane burrows in my head,
And life is different. The pastoral heart
Has stopped, and in its chambers lies congealed
A limpid afternoon. Surely it is
An afternoon we took our paper route,
The desert primrose of the Afterschool
Softly opening on us as we hurled
The folded news of arson, theft and ruin
Against the vague screen doors of bungalows.
Though fierce dogs sprang like dirty jokes
At us from houses where they never paid
Their bill, you never quite believed the news
We brought. You read the news and thought:
"The boyscout prince will triumph in the end."
In the field of afternoon you paused to hear
The locust make rachitic obsequies
To Sycorax. And then you went to seek
A palace for a democratic prince.

American, you came of course upon
The ruins of Eden where once another
Princeling came. His name was Alexander. Here
He saw the black pools of petroleum
Like evil broth seething from the earth.

Afraid, he made a sacrifice to Pallas;
Then, sacrosant and cruel, pressed on through Persia.

But you remain untroubled, lolling in
That city anchored in the metal blood.
Only an American could bear the scene
That frightened Alexander. Prince, prince
At last. Your palace hangs with bats by day
While all night long wind flings the dry gray hail
Of Asia's poverty against your walls.
About your sleep the beams of empires fall,
And people settle over everything like dust.

# Morels

### (for Norman Arnold)


Because the snow so suddenly fled
We went to look for Ariel
Among the remnants. We found instead
A hill inhabited by gnarled morels.

We gathered and cooked this mushroom Caliban,
Knowing full well he has a cankerous twin,
Identical and sweet to taste, but one who, when
The household sleeps, bids death come in.

Possessed, we thumbed a botany book.
Death was the trap, and the bait
Was life. Like devils we had a look
Of loving everything as we sat down and ate.

Like devils we are punished by survival.
We laugh at each other wickedly,
Knowing that in seeking beauty, we found evil,
Toyed with it—and came away scot-free.

## The Red Flower

I have worn a day now for fifteen years,
And it is not like a memory.
I *remember* other days: the dove gray nuns
Saunter among the gargoyles,
And the air burns between them.
But this day is different.

We are riding at dusk across a glacier,
A white corpse whose skin is broken with blue eyes,
And all the rotting of the world seems beautiful
And its maggots as tender as forget-me-nots.

Snowblind, we enter the cold little valley
Below the glacier, where the horses' hooves
Ring loud not with sound but hollowness.
We pause beneath dark, humorless pines
And look at the meaningless blue-snow-water
Of the glacial brook. Then in the black
Bank-mud we see the small red flower,
Wet and glowing like a sop of pomegranate seeds
Squandered between the anguish of summer and winter.

Year after year we returned; the glacier always
The same, the valley always the same dark valley;
But we never found the flower again.

Yet we always thought we should find it
And we made a garden for it, a rich world
That is always weeded, always empty.

In winter we sought the flower's name
In books; but no one, of course, had ever
Measured that cold corolla
Or pressed the indescribable leaves.

And we, of course, did not ever really
See the flower, but we see it now.

It is easy to see
The unreal emblem of what may come to be.
Or to forget it or merely remember.
But only the hand, staggering painfully before
The mind, and the mind dragged cruelly by.
The hand, can bring the real flower forth.
The mind humbled in a waste of snow.
The hand chastened in a maze of earth.

## The Visible Moments

I think of that poor girl in the tale,
Weaving the shirts of nettle,
Which is a way of hoping that years
And hurt hands may settle
The nature of approximate swans
That seem to fly out like stars
From our lives to be lost
And never understood. Good, but I fear
The story fails to show
The danger of falling in love
With nettles, of thinking the comic sheet
With eyeholes is the naked ghost
That stands in judgment on our lives.

The most visible moments of
My life are the least visible:
An early snow has fallen. My love,
You and I are picking the almost ripe, dull
Grapes of a loved vine. The snow melts
At the tops of the bunches, runs
Like a winter dew into the green concavities.
My hands are changing into agonies
Of change. The winter sap seeps
Up my arm. And when I gaze
Into the rhythm of your face

I know that whatever it is
We are doing in this vineyard
Is fatally forever us.

Or, I hear behind me the sybiline
Whisper-laughter of fire in the kitchen stove
As I see you turned from me in the door.
You wear a pink hat, a thin
Cheap coat, and your legs are so mortal
That my heart weeps with the knowledge
That love is a whirling center, gathering fire
And seasons. And even poverty
Can be counted in its riches.

I know that these two days
Are in some way the same. I know
That I cannot know the way of that way.
But save me from ordering them
By will. Save me from denying them
By symbol. Let them stay a poetry
That refuses to die in the poem.

# Christmas Day at Kom-Ombo

It is not easy to speak of this land:
The shocked edge where the Nile gainsays
And Sahara smiles like loss. A few mimosas
Rise from the banks of canals. The hands
Of gray palms rise cantankerously,
As in a private distance invaded by
A telescope. It is not easy to imagine
Reasons. Beneath the tedium of rumors
Of accident or stupidity, I can only think
The train has stopped here because here is where
Trains stop, sun and dust on their numbers
Forever.
    It was here they say
That Juvenal saw those tribes clash
In battle, and the conquerors bend down
To gnaw the bodies of the dead.
He returned, they say, to Rome, disgusted,
To become the bitter satirist.
They say. But surely they say wrong.
To see one's nightmares catch up with life
And scuttle alive under the impartial
Desert day might move one, but not, I think
In the way of bitterness.
    As for myself, I watch
From the window a few men from the village
Beating drums and playing shepherds' pipes,

Their bodies glancing like flint against
Their filthy robes. And to one side
The thin youth who gazes up silently without avarice
Or vanity at our windows. And then those
Young Americans from the train, each with
His limpid face and his carefully tended patch
Of acne, offer the boy clothing.
A fortune which he refuses, explaining,
As the dancers, the drums, the pipes
Cease, that he is a Bedouin and has
Great pride. For the moment, like the
Entertainers, I am appalled at the
Sacrifice. Finally, the pale glint of
Money, the pride crumbling, the music
Rising again, like breath after a silence
On the death bed. Then without preface
The violent sunset begins, flame combed
Out across the inhuman blue enamel.

I draw no moral, nor should I had I seen
The cannibals. The unrelated
Train for no reason begins to move me,
An irrelevant American, away from the
Bedouin in whose now severed hand is held
As in a nest, the bright, hungry nestlings.

## The Blue Light (after Grimm)

Last night the hazardous soldier screamed
As one by one the playing cards went blank:
The lucky features of the king dissolved,
The retinue of servants disappeared.

In the rich bouquet of bedlam
The soldier wandered, telling a tale
Of a blue light burning at the nadir
Of a well and tied, as by a nerve,
To a dark and grinning slave who made
Of him a conjuror. Here the king renewed
His mystery. The fifty-two lovers footed
The morris dance of numbers where
Discarded deuces cinderella to ironic trumps.

Our soldiers cannot leave their slave,
But they say that they have come into
A place so strange that there is no way out—
And mean that they have entered where
There was no way of entering.

## The City's Meaning

The flower burns the rock. Electric dark
Broods, crouching in the arc
Of heaven, like the brume that grows in glass
Of ancient churches until sun and candle guess
Each other through a *spiritus sanctus* of gloom.

Thus the mantle of Elijah falls,
And, reeling, the spirit cries,
"Elijah, I am ready now for prophecies."

Only the agate eye of noon replies:
"What is prophecy but human cunning
That sees the desert at the city's meaning?"

The serpent eats itself, the flowers char
The rocks, rocks eddy in the purple air.
At the height the humdrum riveter looks down upon
The mirage of love feathering the dunes.

# Notes for a Learned Article

Melville, gazing the courts of the sea,
Beheld young whales arrayed about
Their dams. They suckled and stared beyond
The solace, perhaps into the infinite.

Lawrence, reeling back from *Moby Dick*,
Repeated the trope, and Crane,
Already awash and twisting on the reefs,
Turned to the seal's gaze as to a weathervane.

Whither do these mammals gaze who lull
On the breast which is really an eye,
A great transparent profile where fishes swarm
Like leucocytes, and shadows atrophy?

In the gulf streams eyes disguise
Their meeting in sounds of Tartarus and Paradise,
Promising behind a gauze of foam
To lead Melville back to his ancestral home
And leading instead to some singular perversion
Where water becomes words—and words, immersion.

## The Larch

These fastidious trees will not herd.
Discrete in crowds
Of alders, their thin green
In the green of summer is hardly seen.

But in autumn they become
A society of pallid flame
Like saints reflected in violet air
From communities of children's hair.

Until like saints they cannot bear
To go to heaven but stand in the drear
Winter, a dim whirlwind of nerves,
Smouldering with sparrows and love.

# Sunday in the Laboratory

It is Sunday in the laboratory.
In the aquaria the little newts glitter
Hardly less transparent than glass,
Hardly less liquid than water.
And all my love should press
Through vitreous bars to swim
Like slow light through transparencies
Of glass and water where this quick slime
Draws to its dragon's consciousness
Fire through a gill-ganglion of fern.

Yet all my love drifts backward to
The after-image of that human embryo
The size of a hand and saved in an urn
Of homicidal fluid on a noncommittal wall.
His body is all the stupor of time,
Amphibian haunch and bird crook.
But light does not enter the pale
Opacity nor water probe the seam
Of the useless gill. The delicate face comes
From nothing in the past and is like
Nothing in the present, but seems
A final art, a future, life that denies
Life, the destiny writ in the mime's
Face captured between impersonations.

23

# The Afternoon Suspends

The afternoon suspends, turning to a tundra
Where nothing listens, nothing sings
As the faint rain thins and vanishes
And with it, the syntax of things.

Alone in the nacre of the day
The white magnolia blooms like lines
Remembered from a tragic play
When the play itself is gone from mind.

I do not believe in these white marble flowers,
But I believe in the moment's miracle
Whose madness is so perfected that love,
Amazed and angry, tumbles from the broken syllable.

## Doves and Soldiers

It is in the great roundness of nature
That soldiers, whose hands
Have become the unconfessing gloves
Of murder, come always to the park
To feed the doves.

See, when they toss the bread,
How the doves wheel down in a flung-wave-break
Like those dreamy pivotings that flocks
Of skating children make
Along the invisible round
Tensions of the frozen pond.

And see how the doves rise suddenly,
Turning and falling round
Some ancestral center till they lie
Frozen briefly on the bloodless sky
In constellated lines
Of flight and hunger, freedom and alarm:

Like the whorls that pivot in the palm
Of the soldier's hidden hand.

# The Moment

You know the moment of the city's greatness
By heart: When suddenly a human beauty
Touches the stone and steel and filth,
Transfiguring the wrecked web of the elevated,
The sly, gambling streets,
The fish-eyed buildings,
And the panicky squanderings.

This is the moment when evening
Darkens the hot nest with its wings.
You expect then the kindliest adventures.
The phone will ring jagged with money,
The pallid, down the hall girl
Will brush like snow against your door;
Street games will go mad with joy;
And one pale anonymous rocket
Will rise among the evening stars.

It is only by this moment
That you guess the excellence
Of what has been and what must be.
Those old gods and lost forests
Were the easy, blameless destiny
Dreamed in the docile mind of nature
Before you broke from the dream
To flay the wild heaven with your tragic will.

# The Forms of Blindness

My gilded runner, athlete, my sled,
As down the frozen aster hill we speed,
The crazy bones of ice half-wake and whine
Through your body into mine.
We burrow, burrow in the turning snow.
White above and white below,
Until Polaris fractures into Christmases of green,
And roseate children take me by the hand
To lead me, laughing, home and blind.

And oh, it is just the same in summer
Where I sprawl like some reefed swimmer
In organ chords of sand; opened to a sun
Whose glance times my breast with fossil ferns
And at the dykes of smug eyes prods
Until my head floods with a boredom of red:
I open eyes to find the world has gone
Beneath a sea of milk. I gaze up through this mild
Marine at a small sun: paused, pale, no longer wild.

And oh, is it ever the same in here
Among philosophers' ring fingers, where the air
Stirs with vague migrations north and south?
I stare till, empty handed with truth,
I reach out for snow and sun and then

It is the same and not the same.
I cannot go blind in snow and I feel the cut
Of the sled through a wintry lapse. I cannot find
The sun, and my white smile floats on a world gone blind.

# Arion: An Elegy for Dylan Thomas

Those of us who sit lifeless on the headland,
Gazing at the bottom of the sky—until men say
We are stones—we hear. We hear what wind brings.
We sniff the spoor of pallid tracks in air.

We hear, Arion, how it was for you in Sicily.
At Taenarus when you reclined among
The big white grapes your voice hovered
Above, a virile ghost, remembering
The dithyramb of the poor earth at Lesbos
Where the thin wheat stands like threads
Of light in the passionate forest of poppies.
When the knees of the maidens loosened
Your voice sang of untouchable pines
Scattering gold in the dry clefts of cliffs.
And when your poet's body grew fat with prizes,
When your face turned blue and on you came
Death's geometric visions, the voice sang
That the body of an abacus is too simple;
A crying of wheels is not, as men like to say,
"The terrible complexity of modern life,"
But its bleak simplicity. Life quires
For the craft of pudic eyes. Life, you sang,
Is maddened only by the thing it understands.

We who huddle on the headland at the bottom
Of the sky, hear the truth and can guess the lies.

The bone of the abacus will lurch along its string
And say that sailors, coveting your prizes,
Forced you to leap, singing, into the sea,
Where dolphins, susceptible to music, brought
You back alive to Corinth. But it is too like a water
Clock to say you were saved from death.
The fat poet is dead. What we see coming in
Astride a dolphin is the child of the New Year,
Lean, unknown, naked, all the foliations
Of his divine complexity tightly budded under
The puerile tension of the mystic foreskin.

# In Memoriam: Ernest Hemingway

It is the morning of blankness,
The moment of Idahos.
The instant the grouse saves
Its life in a taxidermal pose.

It is the morning of blankness,
The moment of Madrids.
The instant the roof falls
In flames down caryatids.

It is the morning of blankness,
The moment of Africas.
The instant when silence
Grows like a sky from a sudden noise.

# The Bone House: Analogues to Beowulf
### (For Hal Folland)

I had thought that it would last forever,
These pale waves running under a polar dawn,
In which I seemed suspended vainly.
And no dreams. Only the dawn floating in
And out my eyes. Yet not seeing and yet
No blindness, but rather sight and seen
Awash together in the hollow over which
The wave's brow leans.

            I cannot say this does
Not last forever. If it does, then this
Lasts also: Waves wither after pain.
Then hollow is no longer hollow, but a vault
Arched out like the eye from its natal socket
To fill the socket of the world.

        After
Waves withered, with a cry of anger wind roared
Into the caves. And I was made
Lonely with a name.

        In my father's hall
I crawled, dragging this name across the floor

Between the benches where his warriors sat.
I gazed at their legs, columns of scars
Latticed with leather thongs. It was as if
The legs conversed with secret words.
Sometimes, burdened with my name and stung
By secrecies, I slyly bit the legs,
And though the hair and goaty skin amazed
My wilderness, they told me nothing. At last,
Ashamed and angered, my father dragged me by
My name into a corner of the hall. Thither
The warriors threw their table bones, the staves
Of the boar's hull, the heavy ballast of
The hind's flying cargo. But, the very bones
That bruised, I formed into a wall, and then
A house. At first the warriors grinned to see
The soft white spider weaving his web,
But later they forgot me. And my father
Forgot. As for the queen, my mother, only
When wars emptied the hall did she glance
Toward my house of bones, moving her lips,
As though she half-recalled my name, and half-supposed
She saw me staring through the gleaming bars.

The beast saw me. You know the way of beasts:
They wander the land when the harvest fattens,

When the grape seems to close its cloudy eye.
Then warriors mutter, lie near the fire
As night by night a comrade disappears.
And when they sleep the beast comes in, his face
A veil of whirlpools. For a moment he glances
Through the thicket of bones. He bows and leaves.

The hero saw me. I heard in the hall
How the hero came in a green boat
Bearing a cargo of twelve dead men,
All pale and naked, no blood in their veins.
And when the hero stepped ashore, the boat
Recoiled from land, returned into the waves,
Ran silently against the sea and did
Not rock one bit the twelve who slept, like twelve
White statues of the hero, each one's face
The hero's save a different shadow sealed
Them.
                    In the hall the hero made my father
Old, but the queen grew young. She passed the wine cup
Carelessly, as if a noble guest were nowhere near.

One dawn the hero stood before my cage
And laughed. With amber wit his eye
Played over the airy teeter-totters,

Eerie levers and lapped-over cross work.
Then with one droll finger he disturbed
One bone and all collapsed. "Come," he laughed.
In a clearing the beast was waiting, and though
It was the hero drew his bow, the beast
Entrained his face to mine as if to warn
Me. When the arrow pierced him he touched
It foolishly, and with his fading face
Still turned to mine, he lay down clumsily.
The hero cut out the quaking heart
And held it like a frog, briefly, gravely; then
Squeezed the blood into a basin. "Drink," he said.
As I drank, the hero spread his arms
And I saw him change into a tide
Of blood washing round a phosphorescent cross
Of bones, but these joined marvelously. The great,
The subtle house!

         And when the members of
The hall came up I was alone with the beast.
They called me "hero," and the king feigned joy,
Begged me to stay in the place of an evil son,
Long since dead. And the queen, my mother, feigned
Indifference, her eyes following a quaint bird
In the hands of a tree. But I, burdened now

With still another name, remembered my crew
Of twelve white sailors, resting on their oars,
And I knew that I must find them, and I set out
To do so. Like my mother I feigned
Indifference and turned my steps inland, away from the sea.


## II

No season staggered on the wizened land,
But twice the thunder dragged its chains,
And once, with faceless columns sweating fire,
Aurora borealis dragged the landsend
At my eyes.

No season staggered on the wizened land,
But I rose, dragging my chains across
The hardened field. I walked, the gristles in
The sockets whining, the kneebones in
The dice box clacking, wind and waltzes
Howling in the bellows. And I came
To the house abandoned to its fear:
                    The door
Is locked open; black shafts of emptiness
Well from pavid windows. Whey-faced marsh-mist rides
The rooftree; farmer, wife and child have fled.

Yet I came to lie in the darkness of this house.
To wait, to listen for the mourning footsteps on
The roof; to wait at last the shadowed face
Hanging batwise at the doorway; then
To rise and finish with the adversary.

He was godlike. His calm fingers tried
The seams between my ribs. I was human;
My fingers ran to his throat. Godlike,
He would free my breath. I would prison his.

The house trembles as we wrestle. It cries,
The beams bend, groaning on our silence.
He drags me like chains outside the door,
But I have the strength the gods refuse:
Madness mutters at my wrists and I feel
Him slacken in my hands, go sick and weak
Beneath my knees. But it is just then
The clouds part and the moon shines through,
So that I see suddenly his open eyes.
And as I gaze I sink down through myself.

Seraph fading in the rubble
Of chaos, touched by bubbles
Like half-formed lips; strummed by bands

Of minnows, like fingers, willing themselves hands!
All the tutored parts of me surrender
To Old Night. Arms go separate ways.
The brief friendship of cells is sundered.
Voiceless I float among whispers of a voice:

"Because you have conquered, the house is yours.
And, because you have conquered, your strength
Will be greater than any other's strength.
But, because you have conquered,
Your strength will be less than it would have been."

And all at once I am alone with the world
And conscience. And I see the season on the land:
Snow is blowing like a hissing ghost into the sun.

### III

Inland, inland wandering. Name on name;
And knowledge of weakness under knowledge
Of strength; and weakness heavier. This undersoul
Hung like my reflection in the opaque earth.
One moment all was air and the blinding glimpse
Of everything; the next, I spied this shadow
Body, head down in another world.
There was no more walking on the hard earth then.

But down-diving in an atmosphere
Of monstrous sunset where the sun denatured
Each thing evenly with olive light.
In the briars of this land swam beetles
Whose hot omnivorous eyes were hunting all
Too cunningly in pairs. Yet in this sullen
Light these eyes appeared at times to soften,
Twinning like the bonny rosefruit on the rose.
Watching them I began to move this way and that,
Like hunger without object; again to pause;
Again to move, but always following
The cunning torches of my hands. Saffron and carmine
Were these torches and each finger sheathed a lilac nerve
That had no memory, yet murmured of
A future valley.
                    I came at last into this valley.
A valley cinctured by the lace of thickets
Through which the level light still stared,
But, broken in the meshes, stretched in slender
Cornucopias of color. And every
Color trained upon a distant mead hall standing in
The valley's center, very pale, its windows dazed.

Toward me through the streams of color
Came the manor's lord with retinue.

The lord smiled. "What clever hands you have,"
He said, "for all the rest of you is bleeding."
He led me to his smithy, "Make a sword,"
He said. My hands had never known metal,
Yet they made the metal neigh, then soothed
Its anguish in the tongs. I gave
The bridled metal to the lord. "A good
Blade," said my master. Then he laid
Its edge against the tendon of my heel.
It sank in silence through the cord, and I
Was lame. "A pity," said my master, "yet
It was the sword, its edge and weight alone,
That cut. If anything, I held it back.
But now you will not want to wander.
You will be a good smith in a priceless
Smithy, banquets of gold reeling in your hands."

For a time it was true. I built with gold
And silver, steel and bronze, as once I built
With bones. Eerie houses with chambers of pearl
I made my master, who took them with
A smile. Sad manikins who wept for fathers
I made his sons, and a man of brass
I made to guard his house. And as

My master smiled at each new toy, my lameness
Pleased me more. But then the dream came upon me.

I dreamed I told my master's sons to walk
Backward through the snow toward the smithy, there
To have a precious gift, and when they came
I slew them and fashioned from their skulls
Twin goblets for their father. I dreamed he sought
Them, finding only tracks leading from my forge,
And leading to his hall as though himself
Were murderer. And when I woke I looked
From my door to see white mold had formed
Upon the earth and at a vast and wistful
Distance the sons were walking backward.
I turned to the forge, hammering all
The partly finished toys together with
The partly finished swords, and I watched
The two boys backing toward me in a sleepwalk.
And just as they came to my door the wings
Were finished, and I rose screaming above
Them. Then I soared, the lame man in the sky,
Fleeing a dream of vengeance for the laming,
Fleeing the weight and edge of a sword
Of my making. And higher than the air.

Yet the dream had wings, too, and murder
Backed upon me still. I flew faster.
Faster, faster, and into the source of light
I beat. And then as I was turning
Into light itself, bending along the bow
Of heaven, turning in my speed to pure light,
I heard the voices of my myrmidons.
And I was walking on the hard earth in the dusk.
And the sunset, the color of the rose fruit,
Showed the origin of the song. I no longer fled
But limped toward the rose and the singing.

IV

Athwart the way my father's mead hall stood,
Betrayal squinting through the doorway. Where
My father once had sat and given rings
To guests sat one who wore my father's beard
And costly lips and eyes. And yet I saw
The face submerged beneath this face—old shark
That still swims up the vertebrae and gazes out
The hollows of the skull.
                    My mother:
Her glance, like a white butterfly, careened
About the air. And seeing me, she loosed

Her voice, as though she freed a sparrow hawk
Into the room and, beating round the walls,
It screamed, "Revenge your father's death."

It is the way of usurpers to ring
Themselves with power. When they shake their heads,
Entranced, their warriors shake with them. And yet
This power is their ruin. They can never flee
Their strength. On land it walls them round
And in the quicksands drags them down.
Miles beneath the nests of meadow larks
They sink and settle inch by inch through stone.

As for this usurper, luck was on
Him yet. His warriors quivered when he shook
His head, and seizing me they dragged me from
The hall and bound me naked in the woods
For wolves to quarry. Dark was my grotto.
When evening came at last, this grotto was
But little darker. Darker not, but louder.
Louder not with sound, but preparation,
Like the tensile body of a lute
When lutist's hands draw near. And then
The first long icicle of sound. The song
Began, the wailing far away of wolves.
The lute was struck. The minstrel now must finish,

Let the net of music spin and tighten.
But the wolf who entered the grotto
Was no stranger. Wolfish wariness did not
Conceal my mother, nor did glittering fur.
She gnawed my bonds and freeing me, leapt back,
A bitter creature formed for bitter work.
"Run with wolves," she moaned, "and learn their way.
There is no other way for you. And when
You learn their way, revenge your father's death."
Then she wheeled and ran. I followed her
By sound until I came into a clearing gray
With moonlight. There I found a wolfskin, wept
And put it on.

I learned to pace the deer that has nowhere
To hide, and tire it; learned to run between
The rabbit and his lair. The tendon of
My leg was healed by running. Memory
Itself was healed, and only when the moon
Came on us full did we remember
We once were human. Then fear came also on us
And we ran to prove us wolves.
We ran in autumn like a ragged scythe
Across the shadows of the beech trees, and

In winter glided over burnished vales of moonsnow,
And in such silent places that the silence
Killed the sound of breath and turned the mousey
Paw-shrieks back to uncut silence.

Sometimes I think
My mother ran with us that winter.
I seem almost to see her at my side
In silence turning the treadmill of the world.
Certain it is that in the choking spring
She came to me. And it was
As if I saw the painful beauty for the first time,
Staring at me from her ruff of fur.
And then we cut from the pack and ran
On pathways hot with memories toward
My father's hall, and only tarried in
A moonlit clearing where we changed our wolf
Skins for the clothes of humans.
                    At the hall
She drew me past the threshold, where the king
And retinue were sleeping on the floor.
"In drunkenness," she said, "in drunken joy.
And now while the wine burns along the veins,
Avenge us both, my son."

I looked into
The face of our betrayer. Eyes closed,
This face was only the face of fathers.
And I would have run away except my mother said,
"You know the way."
                    I knew the way. I piled the benches
At the door, insanely interlocking them,
As once with bones. I took the brazier from
My mother's hand and broke it on the lintel.

Outdoors we watched the climbing flames
And heard the first high scream. One clever man
Might have escaped, but all that heavy power
Went mad and filled the doorway, bellowing,
And soon was silent. When my barrier had
Burned and only flames stood as a door
Among four walls of fire, I touched my mother.
"Let us go," I said, "for this is done."
She wandered to the door and, facing me, replied,
"My place is with my master. Women may
Not wander masterless, though their masters are
Betrayers." Then she turned and wandered through
The door. Her girdle and her hair rose up
In smoke and flame, and she was like a flame.
And then a flame.

By morning nothing stood
Between me and the dropped eyes of the headland.


v

At the headland I found people gathered,
Weeping. "Why do you weep?" I asked.
"We weep the hero's wounds," they said. And I
Looked down at myself and saw my wounds.
The bruises of the bone house, the crack between
My ribs, the tendon like a drunken mouth
Agape, and flesh, like wattles, hanging where
The wolves had torn me when we ran through nights
Now turned to white sweeps of unremembering.
Then a subtle darkness began to grow
Within the sky and sea as though some vast
Dark body, far away, were walking toward
Me, plucking suns like grapes and eating them.

Darkness meandered patiently, yet always
Drawing nearer. Dancing in time with pulses
Of darkness, which brightened daystars but to
Devour them, the people, keening, circling,
Gathered driftwood for a pyre and piled
It high upon the headland. Then darkness came

47

So close I felt it staring like a bitter lover
Through the dying vines. The wind stopped. And even
The inner spinning of the air was stilled,
And tide ceased.

              When the pyre was lighted,
The vague, glowing tendrils curled over
This last bone house, rising finally to vines of fire
Which were the only light and growing left
Within the world. And through these forlorn flames
I walked and passed into the darkness. Down
The cliff, now changing into air and through
The air now changing into dust I walked.
But, even as I thought, 'all things are turning
Into one thing, and that thing nothing,'
I saw, illumined by the brackish fire behind
My back, a naked hero coming toward
Me. Face to face we floated in the sagging blank,
And I do not believe what happened. Two
Things happened. Passing him, I sank in no
Direction till I came into the boat
And fell asleep with sleeping comrades.
But in truth I also turned and climbed
The cliff again and stood before the pyre
Where something wild was burning in

The driftwood nest. Wild sparks sprang
Like stars into the darkness from that pyre;
Green as joy, red as sorrow were these stars.
Suns arose and little wicked satellites
As well, and turning in the air
They pressed the great dark body back.
Heaven slowly rose again above me, like
A great house. Later the snake of dawn,
Slow with cold, glided round the margin of
My eye. And I saw another day had come.
And I was willing for the day to be.
I was willing to build the house again.

# Poem Without Theme

A queer mist stands from the sea today,
A queer color like the primary blue
Supposed but never limed in the environs
Of certain children. It slants all mute
Things toward their deepness.
The cypress darkens. The wafery city pales.
The Byzantine forts on the hill
Grow young again, calm castellations of
Vague stony gold, squinting through ennui.

But-of-course, the wall between me and
A supreme cadence has momentarily thinned.
Surely, even the faces eroded by greed
Will be transfigured by my vision.
I am deceived. The waiters still run
With their brass trays through the street.
Greece is only as Greece for them is,
A nightmare wrapped in a damned arithmetic.

I see for a moment beyond the world,
But I cannot reach the world's themes. I know
That yesterday somewhere to the north
Another rocket rose and, with the precision
Reserved for madness, followed its nose.
But I do not know what light touched it on the way,

And my only words for it come from newspapers.
My filaments stretch in the blank humus
Of the world, searching a nourishment,
A theme like a fruiting body. I find
The merest syllables. From the darkness I cry,
"See the blue mist, people. See the blue mist."

# Dodecatheon

Far to the south the sensuous life
Of the Mediterranean, paced by leopards,
Moves among the olive trees. *There*
The skin stares through clothes.
*There* the precocious blood stares through skin.
But this north shore is Aristotle's Aegean.
The disparate pebbles draw back with
The tide, counting themselves.
"I, I, I," they mutter wearing themselves to a round proof.
And rapt Demetrios, who believes himself very moral,
Cries, "I—I, but the temptations
Today! Greater than ever before!"
I know better than to answer. I remember
When once I doubted his theory
That tall girls are the best a-bed,
His saying with incisored triumph,
"Ah, then, you have tasted *little* girls?"

Behind us rise the thousand churches built
Like exorcisements on the pagan stones.
Like a thousand beehives they squat in the hills,
Chips of the old gods' acanthus daubed into
The fretting brick which, no matter how stark
The day, finds a moment in which to glow garnet.

Then something flexes in those dim inner cells,
Like eyes moving behind closed lids.

Across the snow-dimmed bay the snow-bright
Mountain called "Olympus" stares forth with
The white feel of blindness.

But the mountain is not blind. It is I, I. I
Am blind to the twelve elegant gods remotely
Scheming against each other with beautiful smiles.

I see only the bold, the reckless preference
For the one expensive God who breaks our souls,
Demetrios, in these twelve parts which plot against
Each other in the muttering tidal drag,
Suing for a unified field, some sweet order,
As all hell breaks loose.

And then you follow the green
Fingers down the darkening arroyas,
The acid mists, to whatever home
The wise thief has stolen for you.

This is the house where the metal
Of life runs like water in dust
And where your son, like Hermaphroditus,
Becomes half girl in the spring of love.

But in the last room you laugh. No artist
Can catch you, but the crude Herm,
Pawky as a milestone, is you. You strum
In the artist's wall, more green
Than his leaf, than his stem
More brown.

# The Aegean

As I swim I feel the tentative rapture
Of a school of minnows flaring
About me. One moment all touch,
Then suddenly fled, a patch of dark tremble
Blowing out from me like a storm.
I turn in the cool, vicarious minerals
And dive, imagining this sea, which coddled
All the vulnerable oddity of life,
Loves life. But as I sink toward the nexus
Of sunlight and dimness I feel
Some rhythm that is neither tide
Nor wave but like an inhalation
Followed by a delicate jet.
Perhaps I see rather than feel
Where the sullen withdrawal of the depth
Spits forth a bright chain of seed bubbles.

Whether I feel, see or whatever, I know
The sea is not thinking of life
But of longer accident and
Stronger synapse. It is thinking
But it is not thinking thoughts.
It remembers but it does not remember
Memories. And thought and memory

Begin, as I drift deeper, to change.
I begin to forget the two great men
Who swam here before me and who almost
Thought as they had been taught
By their supreme teachers. The one
Twice betrayed his Athens because
He had learned to know himself better than
Anything else. The other learned to know
The world piece by piece. Piece by piece
He devoured it.

But then my heel finds that little ray fish.
Thoughtless poison climbs the nerves.
Feeling winks out. Then pain!
Not wisdom but pain brings me
On this shore where in the noon cliffs
A hundred children, here undressing,
There defecating, scream like gulls.

Nauseated by my loyalty I pray to this candelabra
Of children clinging to a cliff that will never
Want them above a sea that will never
Love them, glowing there in a sun that never
Intended them, each one an Alcibiades or

Alexander soon to traduce the wisdom given him,
Soon to betray and sack the world. Each saved
From heaven by the mindless fish that waits
In the depths to sting him to the quick.

# Sailing to Brindisium

This final, night-housed sea revolves
Beneath the stationary ship, taking
Into itself even the engine's too perfect pulse.

The moon has set, and now the sea itself
Is setting on Corfu; setting by rising
Like a puritan wall above that passionate life

Of Greece. A life where laws intensify
To Creon's cruelty; reason to Ismene's logic
Drone; and love to the bruised eyes of Antigone.

And I think of those who always haunt this solemn
Time-killing voyage. Brooke in Skyros; Byron with
His brave tourist verse; and Virgil, whose column

Now rises from the Italian shore.
Their epitaphs agree they died
In fevers, but tell us little more.

Fever, then. What greater fever than to see
Art lose its old intensifying role
In a life that burns as hot as poetry?

And surely they slumber well after that bright
Island sun, that incestuous swamp, that villa.
Who sleeps with a poem all day does not write it at night.

## The Cafe in Salonika

As I enter the cafe, I feel
The atoms have been re-arranged.
Then I see why. The tables are crowded
With youths, whose faces momentarily
Train to my entrance with the perverse,
Self-immolating smile of an animal
That wants to be loved by a human,
Or a human that wants to be loved
By a god.

The atoms sublapse. The boys
Return to their food and jokes, and I
Remember that an Athenian ballet troupe
Is pausing in weird Salonika on its way
To Istanbul. In the cafe's dry wariness
Some are arrogant with beauty and each
Has his lover, yet all turned, bewitched
And hopeless toward a stranger in a door.

My wonder strains the atoms again, and I see
The dancers stretched from Athens to Byzantium,
Their hands fused as their bodies move
In the monotony of their dance.
They move with the monotony of mere life
Across the silted ruins of Thebes and Philippi,

Their faces staring like pale asphodels
From the baking earth. In the roofless mosaic
Of their eyes, Byzantium becomes again
That crude child's drawing of a city
Of two towers and the wall with the immense doors.

Saint Sophia, O lady of holy wisdom,
Now if ever redeem the name we gave you
And open your doors for our mindless dance,
Our belief without hope, our child's drawing.

# The Bee-Eater

The leonine sea pounces
From its wavering ambush
Upon the red ramparts of the land
Where its paws dig caves.
Athwart its yellow eyes
Its white breath stands up like columns.

Here I carry my birthday
Money, misered, wadded, pocketed,
Fingered by a nerve prophesying thieves.
Here I walk, expecting as usual
To buy the friendly toy
That is better than friends
With the old young money
Wet in my hardening hand.

I think I am safe from thieves
Where no one else
Would walk, where I think
Only this anxious sea plays
His metaphysic game. Until suddenly
Before me flies the bee-eater,
The cold, green blue migrator
Who makes no sound, never
Glances, has no curiosity.

But appears, disappears across
The trough of the tricksy world
Like—. Like? Ah, he is
Himself, can have no name,
So may as well be called
Something as absurd as "bee-eater."

I cannot say to him, "Be thou me,"
Or "Numbed by your song, I am you."
For, unlike nightingales or skylarks,
He has no price and will not pause
To take the birthday money we anxiously guard
Because we anxiously want it stolen.

And so, as he sweeps from
The sea and up the red cliff,
His color never counterfeiting another,
I cry at him, "In spite
Of your blue green confidence, bee-eater,
I shall maintain my beautiful despairs."

# A Letter to Pausanias

I pause on a headland. It is clear
Once a temple shimmered here.
Yet the abandoned trench
Of some unknown archeologist
Is as lost in the past
As the shrine's tell-tale fundament.
Rains have rounded the sharp intent
Of both. The little knuckle-print
Of goats' feet weaves a democratic flower
Over what god and what scientist.

At the peak above, a radar tower
Stares, an aeropolis of wire and fear,
Aluminum absence, already never here.
Already its burning fragments drift
Toward rest in this cleft
Where even the great endurer,
Autumn crocus, fails, and goats find
Nothing but a thoroughfare.

Even so, I am unalterably here,
And that shepherd who glides
In Lucretian distance between far sycamores
Will sooner or later come here. Whether
By friendship or suspicion is no matter.

And no matter what hidden god,
Lost knowledge or burned future
Has been dragged here by the other.
Our words shall remind the dead
That only life is alive and that we,
Not they, are the play to be played.

## Prospect from Rhodes

To gaze from an island toward Asia
Is to feel the disguises of God drop
Slowly over life again. Whatever
Is near dazzles, acts, saves. Black
Print crawls like smoking ants on white-
Hot paper. Leaves come like sticky
Babes from trembling stems. Land
Oozes saffron to the sea, out, out
To where whatever is a little distant blurs.
In such numb reaches foam marries gulls,
The sky thrusts ragged dadoes of pallor
Into cobalt calms: Until in true distance
The mountains, as lavender as space, half-turn
Like echoes toward each other. And I care not
That now all civilization grins into the paranoic
Glow which washes backward from the future.
This moment and place which brought Athena
Full grown from a musky boy-God's loutish
Mind is building her temple again.

# A Letter from Crete to Delphi

Three simple schemata
Three elegant models
Three configurations.

The carob trees are the form
Of the wind. Like iron filings
Dusted on paper over a magnet
They translate a daimon.
The heavy trunks and clumsy branches,
The dull, fleshly leaves—each
The antithesis of air—together turn
Profoundly from the sea and
Lap, purl, breathe over the earth.
Though no wind blows,
They are the wind.

The far hill village is a form.
Like the absurdity of our skeletons,
Its geometry enjoys
Its carelessness. The whitewashed cubes
Ascend beyond any meridian, bemusing the sun,
Ascend and give themselves what
No geometry can give itself: a name.

The sea is the sea.
Its greenness at some outpoint
Becomes its blueness.

Its flatness rises,
And from the finishedness of its horizon
Sweep the plunging arcs of its horses.
Like far dolphin, like black loping rainbows
That become at the shore
The multiplicity of the rainbow.

As I send to the world
These things, which are
As they are, I think
Of those who will hate
Them. Those who seek
A vision in the chemistry
Of oracles. The smoke of a
Strange herb caressing the lung,
The needle in the vein, the
Pupil dilated until
Weeping before light it owls
Through the night stopes of Saturn.
But I send these things,
Which are as they are,
With esteem and a friendly question:
If the dream of the pythoness is a lesser
Beauty, why bother? Or if it be
A greater, how is it borne?

# The Statues in Athens

(During the excavations of the agora of Athens, a bit of broken pottery was found on which was written: "Eumelis, come as quickly as you can, Ankesimos.")

The archaic statues,
Remote in their bliss, stand
Among themselves in the dark museums.
They survive.
The hands at the thighs with nothing to do.
The dawn-like foot forward, the smile
Like a spell fixed on the waver of chaos.
And they survive.
Far from museums they survive.
In the gray layers of the river silt among
The fallen columns they smile forever.
And in the sea they smile up the darkness
Below the faltering well-shafts of the moon.

But they survive so well that
It hardly matters if they
Condescend among us.
Not they who will survive us all
Drive me, shaking, into the summer night,
But the faceless shard on which

Ankesimos the workman scratched,
"Come as quickly as you can."

Ankesimos, you were sly and cruel. Goats' hair
Sprouted in the impure marble of your
Thigh. There is no statue of *you*.
Your ordinary stink, your clumsy misery
Did not survive, but they endure
As I hasten to you twenty-five centuries late.

# Thasos

Far from reasoned Athens, this acropolis swings
Above a sea seen green and brook-root-purple
Through a cartography of pines.
The massive stones lie together not quite like
A suspended sigh, but, yes, as though something
Mild, vague, sad had entered the rock from the stone dresser.
As though the most human atom had entered the least.
In the cliff, footholds mount to the shrine
Of Pan, footholds for the horses whose gashed necks
Bled into the mindless God's basin.

Later as we drove toward the village at night, the headlights
    caught
That ragged boy who needed a ride.
He was too cold and shy to want to talk,
But he said that in his sack he
Carried some clothes and a little bread,
That he was going to sleep at an uncle's house
In town. And so, it seemed, he had
Those three things which my child's geography book
Had said were the needs of man.
But why was he so late in the mountains?
His work, he said. And what was his work?
He said, "*Me zoa.*" With *life?* He was working

With life? But no, the language had tricked me
Again. "With animals." He was a shepherd.

If he were clever, I guessed he might always have
His food, clothing and shelter, and if
He never let himself think of anything else.
But I, still wondering what
It might mean to work with life,
With *zoe* rather than *zoa*, *anima* rather than animal,
Saw a white horse bleeding in
The altitudes of dusk.

Could it be that if you work with
Life, you die? Yes, that was it.
You die, you die literally.
The naked spirit opens
Its noble but foolish arteries
In a marble grotto high above
A tender, illiterate sea.

Later in America
I could not imagine
Why I thought this was so.